XI

A Collection of Poetry on Being Human

Written by:
Andrew Joseph Zaragoza Jr.

Dedicated to Marian, George, Consuelo, George Jr, Pal, Claudia, and my sisters.

Thank you.

Being Human—101

Culmination—I

Foreword

I have literally known Andrew since the day he was born. He showed many creative impulses at a very young age. He was encouraged by many special people in his life to strengthen and learn about his gift. As he grew up, he broadened his artistic talents to music, creative writing and many types of arts. As gifted as he was, he was also gifted in helping others when they needed it. He is wise beyond his years because of good experiences as well as bad experiences. In those bad experiences he learned that he wanted to help others be the best that they could be even when they didn't see it themselves, myself included as he has made me be a better person as well as a better mother. I've enjoyed his writing and I'm happy he is sharing it with the rest of the world.

Claudia

Introduction

For someone who was deathly shy as a child and acted out in rather quirky ways, it's no surprise that I decided to debut this book under the title, "XI." On a scale from 1 to 10, I've always felt at an 11. Eleven has since demonstrated its strong meaning to me after experiencing multiple opportunities for growth, experiences during my adolescent, and early adulthood years. Hence the reason why I want to continue being an inspiration to young adults and the youth. We are in a period of time where there is unlimited access to knowledge at the literal palm of our hands. I find the youth being so underestimated nowadays. We are limitless!

Aside from this, if I had the opportunity to mentor myself while re-experiencing all these raw and uncut emotions, I'd tell him this,

"Relax, life is good. This isn't the first time that someone has gone through it and it may not be the last. Your grandparents are proud of you, wherever they are and whoever they are helping right now, they have not forgotten to drop in and visit your dreams to express how much love they still have for you. I know it hurts and it may seem like it's unending. Sometimes it is. What matters most is how you use it to fuel your future. Use all this raw energy and untapped potential and fuse it into productive, positive, and powerful vehicles for others. Start now. Not only life, but everything, is too short for you to dwell. Ask her out, defy your authority to yourself, and be original. It's the outliers that bring interest and inspiration. Martin Luther King Jr, Albert Einstein, Elizabeth Lofus, Walt Disney, and J.K. Rowling,

have all been through this. Failure after failure, they decided to keep persevering and success was inevitable. And so, you too, will encounter success. May it be in the form of personal growth, professional development, bountiful opportunity, or the experiences that come with mentoring others. You too, will have left your mark on the world. 5 years, 10 years, and so on, may you continue to inspire others with your word and wisdom."

Had I taken the opportunity to reach out to the ones I felt for, maybe my life would have been different. Perhaps, I wouldn't have achieved success as a Mental Health Counselor in the community mental health field and, simultaneously, received my B.A. in Psychology while teaching students with ASD in the mornings. I may have been in a different place and time with someone else, or not at all. Whatever the case, I have no regrets. This collection is a one-part love letter to the past, two-part reflections on my personal growth and past experiences, with some sprinkles of fictionalization. I crafted these works in a way that gave them each a life of their own. Though there is inspiration from myself, the author, I give no more life in the ultimate and final product. That is up to the reader's interpretation, the text itself, and my own.

Maybe I won't have that opportunity to speak to the high school teen that just wanted to be accepted and had slid under the radar for fear of intellectual bashing. However, what I can say, I will. It is my hope with this debut collection of my words, that I reach out to others, inspire them to express themselves unapologetically, and to be unflinchingly honest and genuine with my readers. May they continue to inspire others as a result. This is the community I hope to nurture. This is only the beginning, and so much more is yet to come. I now introduce: XI.

With endearing admiration and hope for the future,

Andrew

Me

Made for LA

I took a drive
To Hollywood
And came across
An empty
Exhibition.

While looking in,
The emptiness
 Yearned to tell
 me
That it still had
Some spirit.

Made for Los
Angeles,
And yet
I am too.

Always have.

Always will be.

Dive

Tears when I asked for truth
Silence when I asked for
sympathy

But when I looked for the calm
Instead I found the sea
Raging and rumbling, we
shared an enemy
Tell me, would you swim
beneath me?

Take a dive into my mind and
Find not five but nine times the
lies
Of the lame frame of life
Tell me, would you survive the
dive?

Beware the kraken that hides
inside.

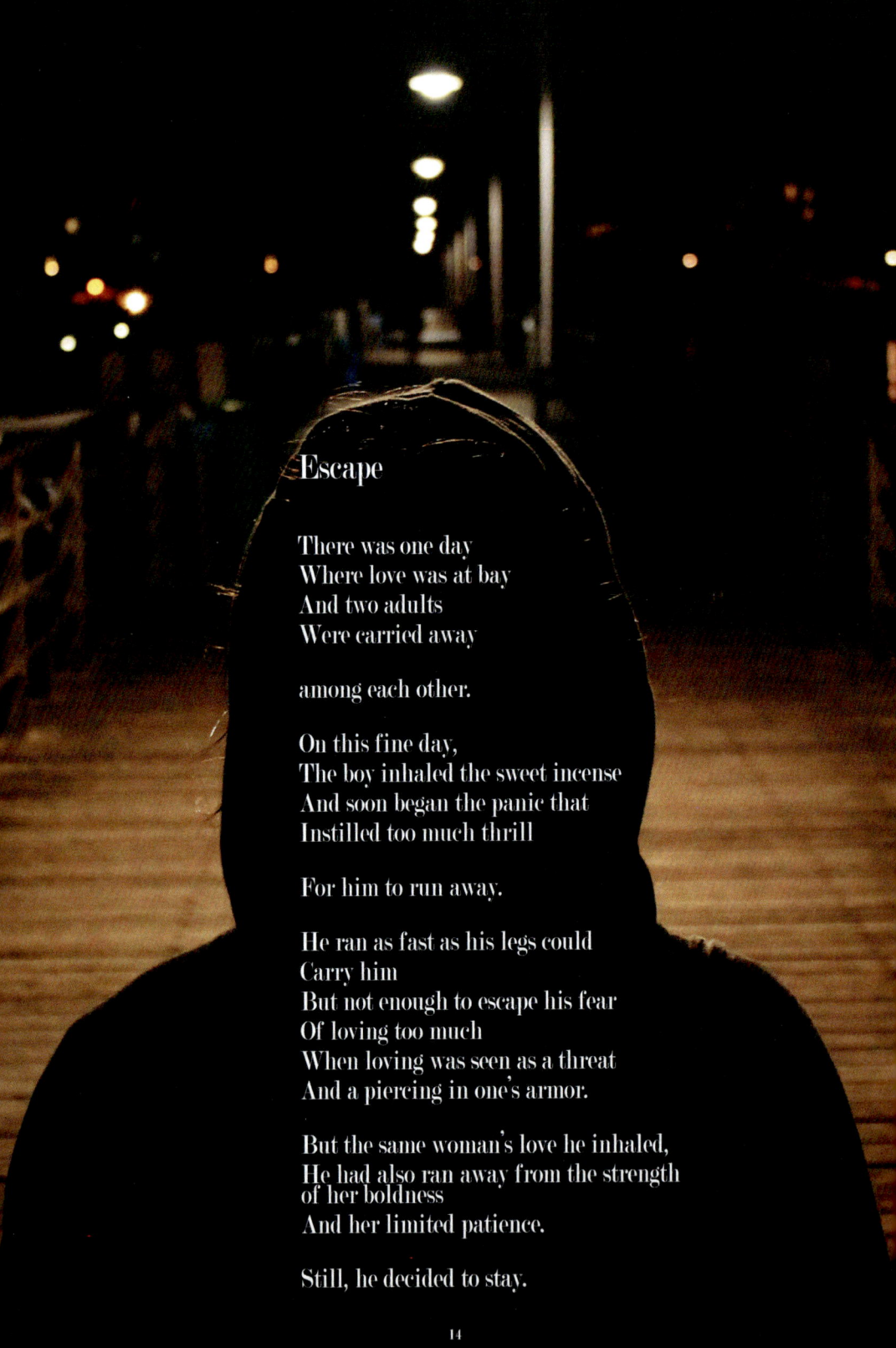

Escape

There was one day
Where love was at bay
And two adults
Were carried away

among each other.

On this fine day,
The boy inhaled the sweet incense
And soon began the panic that
Instilled too much thrill

For him to run away.

He ran as fast as his legs could
Carry him
But not enough to escape his fear
Of loving too much
When loving was seen as a threat
And a piercing in one's armor.

But the same woman's love he inhaled,
He had also ran away from the strength
of her boldness
And her limited patience.

Still, he decided to stay.

ER

I'm patient
As a patient
In a waiting room
Of doom.

Last Ditch

If I had my wish
Like a fancy dish
then I'd act as if I wasn't
Being so selfish.

I'd act like this wasn't
Our last dinner together
After we went our separate ways
To the life we didn't ask for.

I didn't ask to be placed into this world

I didn't ask to be someone's last ditch
Hope for a happy relationship.
I just wished
That I can make this place
Much more of a switch
To happiness

If I had my wish
then I'd hope for this
To be my last ditch
For some small sign of happiness.

Nothing

I have nothing
Nothing to give and
Nothing to take.

I have nothing
I'm sorry but
My house was a
mistake

So you can keep
your cars,
Your clothes,
And your fancy
rake.

Because I have
nothing,
Nothing to give
And nothing to
take.

Online Now

"You've got mail!"
    Hi, hope you're well
    As for me, though I can't tell

It seems,
    As though I am caught in between
    What it means to be seen
    IG...FB...or post a tweet?
    Surely I'm seen, under one
    hundred and forty.

Hi, it's me again.
    4am and I can't sleep again
    The LED's got me weak again
    Or am I overthinking again.

Hi, I'm sure it was read,
    But I'll continue this thread.
    I'm sorry I ran away with dread.
    I should have called instead

Pew Pew

While sitting in the pews
I've fought hard not to use
And think of trying again.

And so I'm here
In the pews
Writing off my sins
With this pen.

Senses

I had a beautiful smile
Enough to light up the night.

I had a piercing gaze,
Enough to see sadness.

I had two ears,
Enough to listen closely.
Until I saw you.

Until I saw you,
I was unable to see in the dark,
Or taste joy in a compliment,
Nor could I remember the sound
of laughter.

The day I found my senses again,
I said no more.

For my lights are dimmed,
My sight is blurred,
And my deafened heart,
Had ceased to hear me out.

Sublime is Not Just a Band

There was a time
Where my mind
Would take me to sublime.

But now,
I travel between days
In a blissless haze
With no control
Over my ways.

The Nautical Exploration

They used to tell me
That the deeper you dive
The more pressure builds

And this is why
Divers wear metal and glass

The deeper you dive
The more pressure builds
Such a beautiful way to die
In that
A plunge can be pressing
The bottom can be bereaving
And the floor belongs to the fallen

They once told me
That the deeper you
Dive
The more pressure

They also spoke of
Mermaids hiding and finding love
At the bottom of the ocean.

And here I am
Still searching
Still swimming.

The Sax's Song

And when the saxophone
Sent its message
To the other side
Of the room,
It was at that moment.

I wanted to become a musician
And play every key
In the sheets
With you and
Your melody.

Heuristics

If you round the
Middle of a number
You get a 5 or
A 0.

Therefore 23 equals
25 equals 30.

You can see why
An old soul
Is what people call me.

Coffee Cup & a Dagger

A coffee cup and
A dagger
Is all I need
To get through the day

I'll need the coffee
To keep me at bay
And the dagger
To pave my own way

Unflinching Tenacity

So I'll continue to write
As it's what I know
When I close all up
And words can't show.

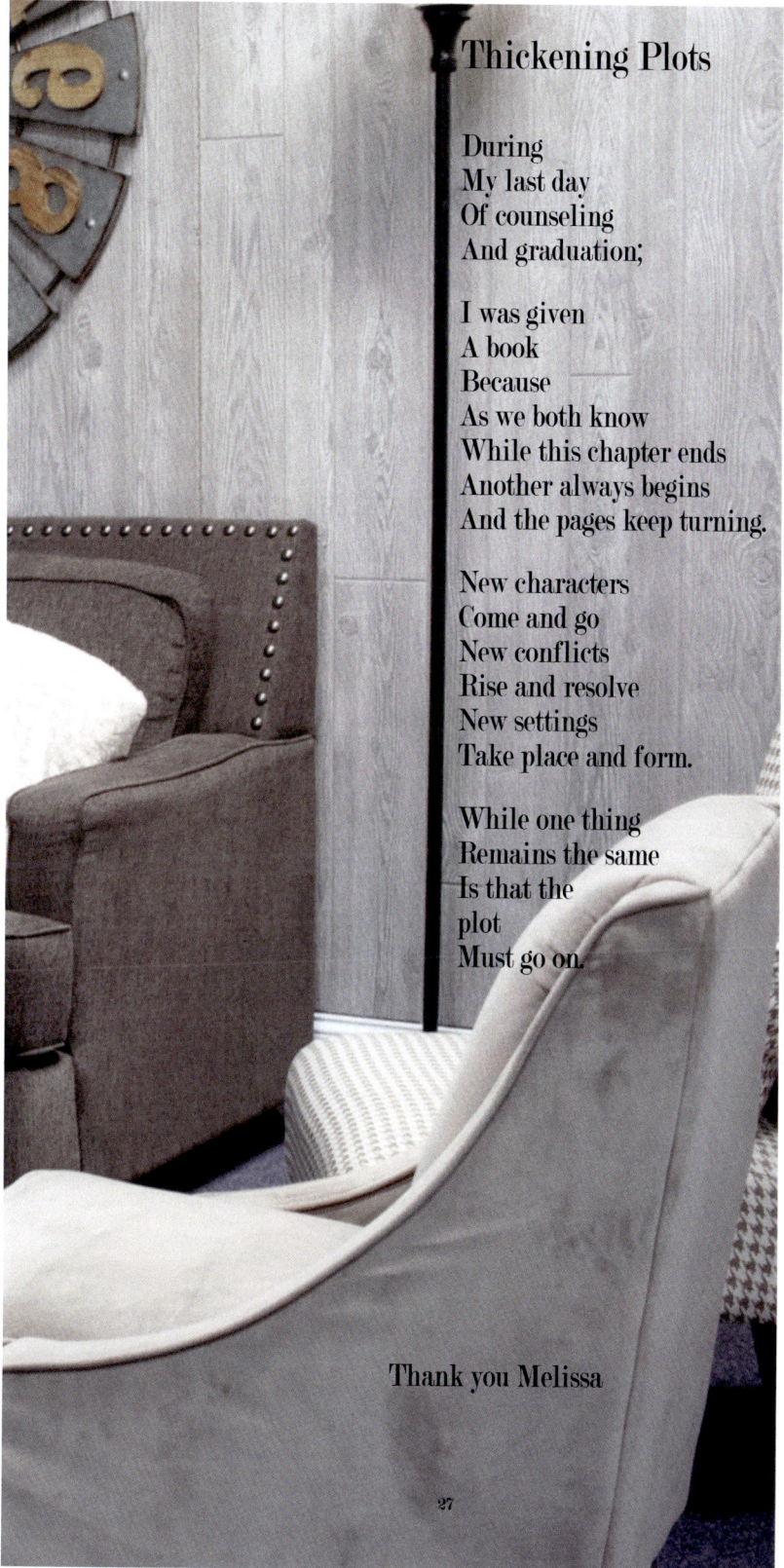

Thickening Plots

During
My last day
Of counseling
And graduation;

I was given
A book
Because
As we both know
While this chapter ends
Another always begins
And the pages keep turning.

New characters
Come and go
New conflicts
Rise and resolve
New settings
Take place and form.

While one thing
Remains the same
Is that the
plot
Must go on.

Thank you Melissa

To Truth

If I speak
Nothing but
Truth
Then I am
Mostly
humbly
A servant
To
You.

Golden Spoons and Doom

If I came from gold
And did what I was told
Then I'd find no worth
In trying.

Because what good is it
That I have everything I need
And I can't see
That there is more than
Just me.

Smiley

Sometimes, I can be
A giant wrecking ball
Of nerves.

And only still,
After everything is
Said and done
Do I still have
These nightmares.

My Promise to You

I can't speak
For you
Or them,
But what I
Can say
I will.

And you will hear
Every. Damn.
Word.

Cracks and Concrete

It's not that I had chosen
A difficult life
With a difficult family
That left behind
An unplanted tree.

But if the roots still grew
More than what water could do
then I'd be fully content
With all of its fruit.

Stray Cat

With every aching day
I've grown to put away
The reason I've been
astray.

Reconciled Circles

They told me
That a great poet
Can say so much
With saying so little.

I guess that's why
I can never know
Where to end the pen
Or know when to begin.

Once More, into the Battle

Wherever my stories
Take you;
Whether it is to new
Heights or expanded horizons,
I can only hope
They bring you safely
Back home to the plains.

Thank you Dad for
teaching me
through story.

With No Intentions

And in the event that I saw you
Just know
That I didn't intend to run away

I didn't intend
For you to chase me
Anyway

So I ran
Just to try it
Anyway

I wanted to run as quick

And painless as possible,
That ceasing to run
Was an unbearable thought

And so I ran
Catch me if you can

More to Me

You are so much more
Than an unplanned birthday.

Let the world fear
How bright
You let those candles burn.

Escape

She went to Vegas
To break away
From the troubles
That came with
Living.

Unfair Treatment

Sometimes,
I'll think of all the people
That have hurt me
Disappointed me
Lied to me
And then
I see that there's more
To my pain and
Their mistakes.

And I'd still wish them the best.

A Boy's Poem

The reason boys
Don't write poetry
Is because they
Don't have much to say

There are no words
That can make a girl
Believe in their
False truths

No amount
Of fast cars
And looking at stars
Can hide their false pretense

No love game
Can retain the heartbreak
Made
By a boy who plays.

And you're worth so much more
Than cheap drinks
And silk sheets.

The reason boys
Don't write poetry
Is because they
Have very little to say.

Choose Me

Though I'm an
open book
With pages ripped
out
And a missing
spine,
I've given you
The utmost
Respect
In trying to read
Me.

41

Me

Please,
If you're going to try,
Go all the way.
Continue far enough into
the past
While staying in the
present
To make it a future worth
finding.

Save me the dread
If you're planning to
leave me
then go right ahead
Because I have no mind
To relive a past
That I escaped
Over many lifetimes.

Please,
If you're willing
To put forth the effort
then I can promise
Nothing but truth
And honesty

And honestly
I can't guarantee
That I'll be forever happy
But at least you can see
That I was always me.

A Mourned Morning

I remember
staring down at you
As you rested deeply
With no intention
To wake up

I imagined what
Your smile could be
Dressed up as nicely
As you always would

And when it
Was my time
To say goodbye,
I couldn't help
But think
That you said it first
As it was most
Indeed
A fair well.

Enamored

Catching Fishes

Remember that one
song?
You'd always play it in
the car
Right after school
On our way to the river

We'd just lay there,
On the concrete bed.
Talking about the future
and
Fish in the pond.
Birds on the rocks
Peacocks in the street.

Sundown came and I
still had
No catch.
The lines kept pulling,
But still no catch.

And you still played,
That same damn song.
Remember?
I do.

I remember
Palm trees and beach
breeze,
Sky ozone and the red
sun,
And that same song.

Press play again
Pause the moment,
Stop me from seeing you
Because I can't rewind
The next months of our
time.

And I never caught it,
The line snapped and I
tied it again,
Only to learn
That fishing and
catching,
Mean two different
things.

By Grace of Gaze

If looks could kill
Then I'd rather live
To see another day.

The Color Purple

It's at this hour
That I've thought of
Nonsensical things.

Like string cheese
And green peas
And the color purple.

Like red shoes
And the new moon
And the color purple

Like red socks
And Lego blocks
And the color purple

Like beached skies
And emerald eyes
And the color purple

And the color purple
Is so much of what
I thought about
That I can't love
Anyone else.

A Laundry List of Love

Love is not
Waiting for your turn
And standing in line
For the next checkout

Love is a fire
Waiting to lash out
When you're not ready
To look her in the eye

It's sitting together
And keeping space
Between the hearts

Love is not
A dire consequence
When you cannot meet

It's baking a cake,
Getting all the measurements
And ingredients
And hoping you timed it right.
Because sometimes it comes out
Too gushy
Or burnt.

Love is not
Waiting for a response.
It's responding to your patience
And having a conversation
With yourself
About who loves who more.

Love is not
A bird in flames
Who's risen from the ashes
To try again

Love is the fall
And the crash
All the same.

The Blind City

If a smile
Could light up a room
Then you'd blind a small city
Into its doom

For someone so powerful
And unobtainable,
The city has no choice
Than to surrender its will

For if the city
Had its way
then no brighter smile
Can bring the day

Own up to your land
My queens and kings
And everyone
transitioning
And divine the shine on mine
And ours

Bring the day back and hide the night
To survive the times that
Surmised our every try.

So only you can bring back the light,
All you need to do
Is smile

It's only right.

Scatterplot

I wish I skipped the paid
ads
To enjoy the good parts
Like being next in line
Or waiting for you
As I put down my name
For two.

I hoped I wasn't too much
When I wore this shirt.
It helped me get through
my first day
As I chased my sanity away
And not much has changed

Nice dress.

Simmer Lover

And it's when you looked at me
That I went ablaze

A blaze that set as
Your anger rose along with the
tides

A fire located long past the
horizon
En captured among the waves
And twisted into a fashionable
Pompeii

Please simmer
Please lower the sea
Because I can't stand
To see the world in flames
As your spirit tides away
In agony.

A Play of Pretend

I'm not going
To act like
The late nights
And the solid car rides
Didn't happen.

Let's pretend
That the end
Didn't come
So soon.

Imagine with me
What we could be
If the lights
Didn't go out.

I never wanted
Best of worst
Only good enough.

The Beautiful View Inside of You

There we were
In the middle of a cliff
Surrounded by
The wind
And our ghosts.

You took pictures
Of everything
Else
Except yourself.

So I took one
For you
Of you
And came across
The most beautiful
View of all.

Happiest Place Unearthed

I found my happy place
within your smile,
and after some drinks.

We began to share more
And let the alcohol speak
About our family troubles

Of course, I hadn't said the best
As you were at your worst,
though i could not help
but admire you, smile through it all

At the happiest place on earth
Was the saddest couple
With no kids
But the cups in their hands.

Lusted by Love

I never was one
To ride
Against the
Tides.

I wrapped around
The pristine condition
Of a deep blue
Sea.

Though no amount of
Lavish lifestyle
Can be
As enticing;
As your ocean eyes
Sink me in.

I never was one
To ride
Against the
Tides.

But with you
I'd ride
Every time.

Sense of Belonging

I was caught between
What I thought belonged to me
Ended up being my source
For insanity.

Tweaks and Twinges

Here we are
Leaving out the details
Of our stories
To better make them
Relatable.

Comforting Words

If it were up to me
I'll tell your dad
That he didn't have to worry
About us and staying
Out past three.

But I'm not your dad
And you're not my daughter
So I'll have you home
At nine thirty.

Blissful Glitch

And maybe all of this
Isn't real.

But I'd still want you
To be my glitch
In this reality.

Full of Pretense

When I dreamt of you
I hadn't the opportunity
To see the beauty
In a false reality.

But oh
It was still
Ever so captivating.

Please

I'm impulsive
And I know this.

But please,
Have patience
For me too.

A Fairy Tale

If there ever was beauty
In my beasts,
then I'd hope
To be happy at least
until forever
Or after.

Postmodern Nostalgia

I'm not looking for
A part-time lover
Or a swipe-right sweetheart.

What I need
Is just what I'll give;
Full time effort
And a love real enough to live.

After High School

As I sit and make sense
Of the world,
I'll know one thing is certain
That you'll never be my girl

You

Believe me
when I
Say
That gold
roses
Used to
Live
Here.

And damn
Do they
Still bloom
Each time I
look —
In your eyes.

Intentional Deceit

I wrote this because
I was in a bad place
In a bad time.

But I'm glad you're here
At the right time
In the right place

With the wrong intention.

Pen Pals

If you had a pen
And read this again
Would you write back to me?

I'm talking
hand written notes,
Drive-in movies,
Taco bell,
And sharing our tells.

Because if it were up to me
I'd bring you back
To 1953
And you'd fall in love
Only once
Repeatedly.

Thank you
George and Marian

Reassurance

There's not much
That I can say
To let you know
You'll be okay.

Except I love you
Any way.

Beer Breath Beach Blues

I choose no one else
To spend the night
Getting drunk with plastic cups
In your car,
Sharing secrets,
Than with you only.

Gatsby Forever

I can honestly say
That when it's all
Said and done,
I'll have my toast
And begin my fun.

Thank you Mom for being strong.

Christmas

And if this is the future I'm given
then I want no part in its present

Stumbling

Self Induced

I spend a whole night
Contemplating the strength
Of a liver
After a full flask of
Japanese Whiskey.

And so I asked,
How do you do it
To which his response was,
Because I hate myself.

2 Cents for your Senses

Sometimes I don't
Make sense
And that's okay.

Sometimes I don't
Make cents
And that's okay.

You

I want to rewind
Everything I've done
And do it right.

But I can't have you there
Because you were everything right
In what went wrong with my life.

A Drink to Remember

How much could you drink
Before you remembered I was
there?

How many unintelligible
words
Would you say,
Before I grabbed your phone
To tell your dad it's okay

He wouldn't trust me anyway

How many more drinks
Before you washed the sink
With tears

Followed by three more beers

How many more drinks
Before you realize
That the pain never drowns
out
As it grows and grows
With each swift.

How many more drinks
before you remembered
How much I cared?

Lost in Spaces

I was an astronaut
Alone in a dark place
Surrounded in water and
Abysmal bliss

While on my travels
I found nothing but
Balloons and flowers
That lifted me up
And scented my senses.

While abroad the mist
And the midst
Of a spacious haze,
I had found an explorer.

They told me I was
In a place;
That I arrived too early.

And so I waited
Until it was my time
To fly.

Lost/Found

Just because I'm lost
Doesn't necessarily mean I want
To be found.

A Filled Cup

Do all of your nights
End up
With heartbreak and heartache?

Enough to move the wind south
And the waves to the west
Without a beat.

Do all of your days
End too soon
And begin as full
As the new moon?

How to Shatter Someone

I love you
I'm just not in love
With you.

Growing Up

Breakfast to me
Was sausage and waffles
Pancakes and eggs
Potatoes and ketchup

So tell me why
That as I get older
The first of day I see
Is bourbon and whiskey

84

Best Friends

I'd rather have the
Company
Of my dog
Than to be
Misunderstood
By everyone else.

Higher Elevation

What puzzled me most
Was how fast you had
faded
The more I became
Faded.

Choice

Sometimes making the right choice is
Not always easy,
Sometimes making the easy choice
Is not always right.

Right?

Kiosk and Kisses

That was your joy.
Getting lost in the jewelry stands
Was as close to peace
As you could get.

I didn't mind
Getting lost with you
As I was never found
In the first place.

But when I held the ring
In front of us,
I can swear
That we were,
Lost no more.

Guidance

Lead the way,
And I'd get lost
In following you
Forever.

Vacant Lots

I'm sorry that
My heart
Didn't make room
For you to stay.

You see,
It left the door
Open for a reason
And too many times
Had they moved away.

Unfamiliar

I was a friend
Before anything else.
I wanted you to smile
When there was no one
Else
To do such a thing.

We had the best of times
Together
And the worst of times
Together,

Until you grew up
And still here I am

Smiling through the worst times
Waiting for the best times
To come again.

As one can only be
Imaginary.

Sunken Ships

I'm not sure
How to navigate
The sea
That we call life.

But I'll be damned
If I don't at least
Try to swim.

Please

Maybe you'll never
Experience
My aches and
pains
The thoughts and
strain
Of a memory
Fighting its way
back
To me
And wreak havoc
again.

But at the very
least
Have some
Compassion
And
Patience
And be
As big as your
heart
Can let you
Be.

Passing Through

So I'll wait
For you to come
See me
And how much
I've grown
Since you've left.

As the doors close
And open,
I'll keep you here,
Always.

Basic Necessities

Some days
Eating
Breathing
And sleeping
Is
good
enough.

Fair Play

I just wish
That giving
me
A chance
Is all that
I can
Ask
Of you.

Cohabitation

To get dragged
Into a world
That I didn't ask
To be in -
Is the ultimate
Struggle
To reconcile.

97

Shooting Stars and Gazing Anchors

If you hit rock bottom,
Keep hitting

Because I know you
Were too brave to give up
From a let down
That came too soon.

So keep hitting
And show them how
A rock
Can shatter a glass castle.

Attack

If it's fear
That fills
You,
then good.

You still have some fight
or flight
Left.

Being Human

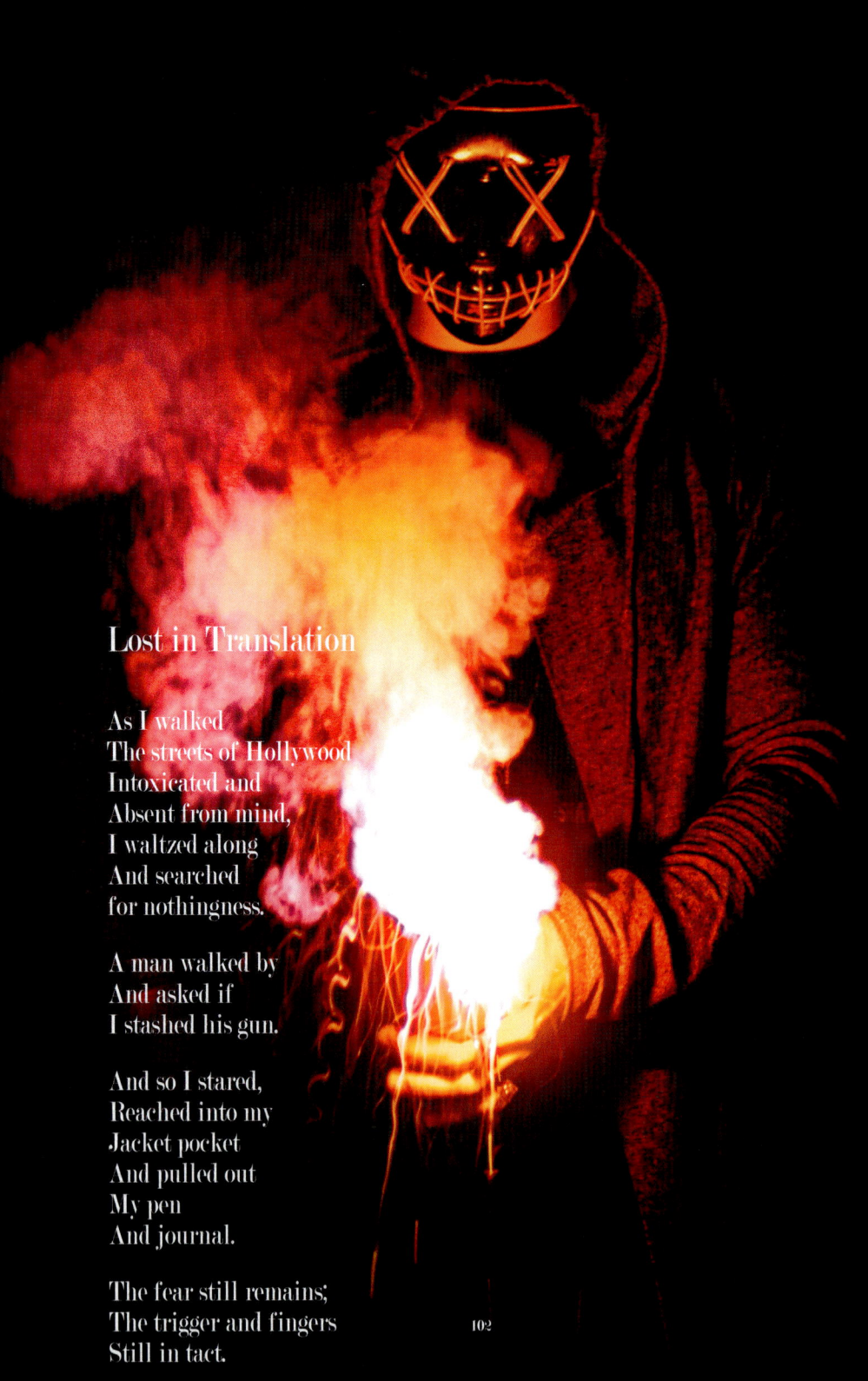

Lost in Translation

As I walked
The streets of Hollywood
Intoxicated and
Absent from mind,
I waltzed along
And searched
for nothingness.

A man walked by
And asked if
I stashed his gun.

And so I stared,
Reached into my
Jacket pocket
And pulled out
My pen
And journal.

The fear still remains;
The trigger and fingers
Still in tact.

Disillusioned

Have you ever
Sat in a room
Full of people
And decided
They're anything
But human?

First to Last

I think the reason
Why we fight so often
Is because some may have
More firsts
Than lasts.

Can you Imagine
What it's like
To be first in line
First to choose a school lunch
Being first to place in baseball
Going on a first date
Sharing a first kiss
Owning your first car
And so on.

But sometimes,

We tend to undervalue
Our lasts.

Like the last ride at Disneyland
Before lights out

Or the last bite of ice cream cookies
And our last kiss goodnight,

Like a last goodbye while they leave
For country
Or from family.

And what about last visitations
And last rites?

Can you Imagine
Our firsts and lasts,
Can bring us closer together?

Dr. Seuss Was an Introvert

Far too often
Am I lost
In thought

But oh
Is it
A place to
Go
And go
And go
Until there's nowhere
Left to be found again.

Management

If it's one thing
That I know for
Certain
It's that there's
Nothing better
Than the
Thrill of it all.

Response Ability

If I was younger
Than I was now,
I'd tell myself:
It's not a race,
And you'll have all
The time
In the world
To still grow up.

An Open Book

The beauty of poetry
Is that
The beginning,
And the end
Can meet on
The
Same page;

Turn the Page

The book is never
Truly finished;
We add our part,
Revise what we read,
Edit what we see,
And retell what we've
heard.

As the pages keep
turning,
So the need to share,
Time and time again.

Your Art

For you
I'll paint the
walls that
guarded you
Into a shade
of
Gray.

Humbly Put

You don't need
To get
The things
You
Want.

However,

You'd most
definitely
Bet your ass
You'll want
To get
The things
You need.

My Wish For You

I hope to see you
On the other end
Of all this.

To laugh with you
Once again
Is all I'd ask for.

Continuously
Until
The end of my days.

What's Always Been There

As a writer
Puts their own world
In perspective,
Simultaneously are they
Tasked
With prospecting ours.

In hopes
To instill
Something that's always
Been there

Only to bring it back
Again and again.

Remember

And just because
We don't have
The same shoes,
I'd still be glad
To walk a mile
with you.

Paged

As new chapters open
In this life,
I've failed to continue on
Because some of my
Favorite parts
Have already happened.

And God damn,
Do I want to
Reread them again,
And again.

Shine on, Your Burning Comet

They told me
That stars
Burn as bright
As they possibly can.

That they are made
From the death
Of others.

That once a star
Forms an iron core,
It's all said
And done

And death has one.

So maybe
This is why
Stars burn
So bright.

In that
Because
They know
That iron approaches
Inevitably.

And yet
They still shine on.

Despite all the iron
That forms within them,
Making others
Take a look
At what they can be
Too.

The Librarian

If God was organizing his bookshelf,
Do you think he'd like our stories?

H20 at Zero Degrees Celsius

I can't believe
Today was a good day

Keepers of the Dreamers

If we are keepers
Of the dead's memories,
then who keeps us
When we die?

Existence Among Us

Did you know
That gold can
Be made by two
Colliding stars.

Two colliding stars
Exhausting energy
Between each other
To provide a force
Like no other.

And yet,

I'm still glad
To have received
My grandmother's
Wedding pendant,
Full of gold
And waiting to shine on.

Tunneled Vision

The more I write
The better these
Pages of life
Seem to make sense

Shall we continue?

It is Written

The reason
We write
Is to create
Temporary escape
continuously.

The world can be
So unfair
And upside down
That we tend to
forget
Our center.

And so
I write for you
To ground
yourself
And get lost
To find yourself
Again.

Just Visiting

I rode out to
The beach
To run away
From my mind.

I kept it at bay
For many miles
Only to park
And have my
Destination.

With my guitar
In hand
And the silence
That night brings,
I played.

Heaven received
A knock from me
And opened
Its doors.

Thank you
For hosting me
In your hotel
For the night.

And even still
I plan for
Check out
To my delight.

Organ

What goes on
Inside
That three pound
bagel.

I can tell you
All about
The stars and
planets,
The Mona Lisa,
The Million year
War;

But what good
Will it do
When you've had
All the answers
In front of you.

And so
I keep searching.

Work

To be
A poet
Is the
Laziest job of all.

I give you
My words
My heart
My soul
And my sanity.

And it's your job
To fill in the blanks
To heal what I
couldn't
To believe when I
can't
And to,clear what I
couldn't.

And so
Only one of us
Pays for it
In the end.

Shine

Candles burn
bright
But stars
Can last
For lifetimes.

Drunk in a Disneyland Hotel

And while we
Layed together
In the hotel
Lobby,
We created our
Home
Right then and there.

Do you see
The furniture,
Next to our bookcase?

Or how about
The entertainment system
Next to our
Fish tank.

Our sofa never
Felt so
Like home
That only one of us
Was pretending
To pretend.

127

Forever

With every
Strength of
My spirit
I will triumph
Over this
Ride called life.

The City and our Canvas

Join me
In painting
Our name
Across the city
That's shrouded
In so much
Black.

An Author's Treat

Sometimes to
End the book
You'll need
To tear out
The chapters
You never liked
In the
First
Place.

Culmination

Critical Thinking Components

This framework of questioning can be applied to many of the poems in this book. An initiative to create further discussion among readers and scholars. Enjoy!

Reflection

1. What is the theme (the central idea) of the of poem?

2. What structural or stylistic technique does the poet use?

3. Who is the speaker of the poem?

4. What is the mood of the poem?

5. What is the imagery in the poem?

6. How is humanity reflected in this selection?

Contribution

1. What are some ways to bring meaningful contributions to your environment and community?

2. How can you bring about change to benefit others and your growth as an individual?

3. How do you think this book instills contribution to the community at large?

4. What are some ways to facilitate contribution to others in your community?

5. When was a time where you felt genuinely appreciative of the work you had done for someone? If not, how could you start?

Inspiration

1. How can you bring inspiration to the community around you?

2. Were there any selections that instilled a sense of inspiration and hope?

3. Who are some of the role models in your life and did they come into mind when reading these selections?

4. If you had the chance to write your own story, narrative work, or collection of poetry, what would it be of and why?

5. Think about a time in your life when there was an opportunity to support someone. What happened? How did you respond?

Reconciliation

1. What are some closing thoughts after reading this collection?

2. Are there any selections that stood out more than others?

3. What are some of the memories or emotions that arise after reading a selection?

4. What new feelings had the selections evoke?

5. In the context of generational, ancestral, or personal trauma, what are some ways to confront them and heal or grow from them?

There is no definite right or wrong answer though it is intended to spark deeper connection in respect to the ideas reflected in this book.

All responses can be sent to andrewjosephzaragoza@gmail.com

Acknowledgments

It honestly feels like an Oscar nomination. First and foremost, I want to to thank my parents, Andrew and Claudia. If it weren't for their guidance, endless support, and giving me opportunities that every parent would want for their child then I wouldn't be where I'm at now. When I had the wildest ideas, they were open and asked the difficult questions when making something a reality. Secondly, as followed, are my sisters. Thank you so much for being patient with me and my wild self. In addition to my Perez and Zaragoza family, each of you hold a special place in my heart and I take nothing but pride in sharing this path alongside you all.

Following the long list of gratitude is my Cali303 family (cali303.com). We've cultivated so much in the past couple of months and this book is a testament to that regarding creative professionals and those in the art field. We are going to accomplish many great things!

Fortunately, I want to express gratitude to the arts and education community that I have been a part of for so long. Without this media that has been here before me and will be here long after I'm gone, this is just a small token of appreciation for all the outlets I've gathered as an artist and educator. Though an ever evolving process, art is never to be finished. I'd want to extend my heartfelt appreciation and warmness to all the educators I've worked alongside with and learned from during my years at the ABC Unified School District and as a student at California State University, Dominguez Hills.

I want to thank my grandparents for instilling in me virtues beyond their life here on this little blue marble that we call Earth. Without them and their wisdom, along with endless late nights of movies and building memories, I would not be as skilled as I am now in my lines of business. May they read this as they rest.

Further appreciation goes out these fellow people that made my project possible. I want to thank staff at Serif for creating an amazing creator's software through the Affinity series. I want to thank the generous artists for contributing their visuals through Pexel, Unsplash, and Pixabay as these messages wouldn't be as powerful without their own crafts implemented.

My last gratitude shout out goes to those who had perpetuated me into opportunities of growth and development beyond my own limits. Without these figures, I would have not known the light without their darkness. Through trauma came growth, I will never forget.

Of course, I thank you. The reader who made it to this page. I wrote this for you to pave your own path and walk the one that was traveled so many times before. Each journey feels a little bit different and, nonetheless, I accompany you in your adventure. May you gain wisdom from reflection, treasure from insight, and an opportunity to be valued.

-AZ

About the Author

 @Graphicsbyandrew

 @Graphicsbyandrew

 Graphicsbyandrew.com

 andrewjosephzaragoza@gmail.com

Andrew Joseph Zaragoza, Jr is a Chicano born and raised among the Greater Los Angeles gateway cities. Having grown up in and now employed at the ABC Unified School District, he spends his time teaching students to become their best selves. He concurrently works with adults at private residential locations as a Residential Counselor. He recently acquired a Bachelor of Arts in Psychology at California State University, Dominguez Hills with plans for post-baccalaureate work.

While growing up, Andrew has become a model to the young minds by inspiring them to achieve their unique and individual greatness. Having persevered through hardships and loss at a young age himself, he found comfort in visual arts and music. Having formal education through several high school art classes, self-taught knowledge, and past experience with the Downtown Art Walk in Los Angeles, he now ventures out to help others through education and activism.

Much of his artistic inspirations come from his grandmother, who first introduced him to a wide variety of media at a young age. With her passing in 2009, he looked to his parents for support and direction about how to proceed with his skills and development. Further, he draws his aspirations from the wide variety of musical artists, Salvador Dali, Seurat, Morley, and more. His style is one of continuous growth and up to the audience's interpretation. He describes himself as the fluid that fills up the audience's containers, liquid and always moving.